Jeff Bowick & Dwayne Henriksen

OPTIONS TRADING CRASH COURSE:

SWING TRADING DAY TRADING AND BEST STRATEGIES

The best strategies to operate in the market in the most profitable way

Table of Contents

INTRODUCTION

When we think of investing in CFD trading or simply trading online, the first thing that comes to our mind is the easy money it brings. So it is essential to study good online trading strategies that work. In fact, it is not difficult to earn with online trading if we know how to adopt the right strategy.

The first question to ask is: What is the right online trading strategy?

The answer is very simple: the winning one!

Although it may seem obvious or even a joke, it is not so. It's all about planning the right winning strategy for ourselves; that's what we're going to talk about here.

It is difficult in fact to highlight a single trading strategy as the best, because as you can see there are several trading strategies, sometimes very successful, but the best is always the one that every single trader finds to suit his style, that is the one that produces stable and profitable results both in the short and in the long term.

It doesn't matter whether you are an experienced trader or a beginner, what we are going to address in this book is precisely the ability to plan the right online trading strategy. We will also present a list of the best known trading strategies.

The first step we are going to tackle is to define a trading strategy.

Basically, we can define the online trading strategy as a set of predefined rules on when and how to enter the market on one hand and on the other hand how to invest in the stock market or in other markets always keeping in mind the money management.

The most common mistake that is made and that you should avoid is to base your strategy on the market, or on the hearsay of other traders, those who have made that choice before you, or those traders who base their strategy not on predefined rules or precise instruments.

We always recommend that you try to learn at least one of the online trading systems, so that you can try to understand and consequently also follow the set of trading rules. To better understand the market movements, choose a broker that shows you interactive charts.

The first point then that we deal with when we talk about CFDs and trading strategies concerns the training of the trader; in this case you will have to go and study:

the different trading basics;

the various trading tests carried out by other traders on the different strategies they have used before you, in order to plan your own.

In fact, a good trader is one who knows how to listen to advice and will thus learn to recognize many more market conditions than he could do on his own. This is the only way he will be able to recognize CFD strategies and profit from them.

So, as you can see, nothing is difficult! Everyone can learn and nothing is as difficult as it may seem.

Now that we've made the right assumptions, how about we get started?

CHAPTER 1   TACTICS FOR BEGINNERS

Which Trading Is Profitable?

There are several basic kinds of options trading activities that the novice and even the experienced traders should be familiar with and get to master their favorite kinds of options trading that it is much going to be profitable during various occurrences. Here are some of the profitable ways.

Buy to open. This involves initiating a new order to secure a new option and eventually getting to improve on the existing trading position as judged from the past trading activities.

Sell to open. Selling to open is selling a specific option that you do not necessarily own and in the end, acquiring a new position or an improved position in the options trading activities.

Buying to close. This is buying a specific option that you had previously sold in the market and eventually reducing a position in the options trading market.

Selling to close. In this kind of trading, an order to sell a specific option is exercised, where whatever you are selling had been previously been bought and end up reducing or exiting an existing position in the trading market.

How to Be a Successful Options Trader

Below are some of the ways we can shine on this options trading field.

Risk management. Life is a risk itself, implying that risks will always be depicted. An options trader needs to master all the possible ways in which he or she can minimize the number of risks that are likely to occur and learn from everyone of it for future good management. For instance, in the capital sector, the trader ought to have a big plan entailing details on how capital should be used strictly. Losses are also part of the options trading aftermath, and with bad capital handle, everything can tumble down. Think of how bad the market volatility can stand, leading to a great amount of capital, and leading to large chunks of losses.

Be the chief in numbers. Options trading involves wide use of numbers. Do you know the implied volatility? Is money in the option or out of the option? For beginners who have no single trace of what is going on, kindly commit oneself to some in-depth research and try to get a spotlight. For the intermediate and experts, keep learning about various numbers in options trading. Life stops once you stop learning.

Possess great discipline. Self-discipline is encouraged as you get involved in options trading. This is the up-thrust motive force that will drive you towards as per your agenda plans with so much determination. You get to follow your specific laid plans and strategies, learn so much from your trading activities, and get the respective skills and experience for more successful options trading. Remember that your set plan strategies are the core objects during options trading, implying that self-discipline will bring you nothing but great success.

Great patience. Every aspect of life is a process led by constant growth. Trade during several market movements and get to learn from it. During this options trading journey, you will be exposed to various occurrences that you need to learn and master each one of them. Learn the possible risks involved, several market tricks and so much on. Well, get the best experience for it is always the best tutor.

Have your trading style. The intended trading style is what's normally implemented in the trading plan. Your trading style should be strictly adhered to and updated with new skills and information as you get involved in various options trading activities. Follow your plan without any other kind of influence and watch yourself grow with options trading.

A trading plans. Failing to plan is planning to fail. This implies that failing will only be reflected once planning does not happen. Successful options traders have big plans. Big plans entail good laid strategies, functions, discussions, in-depth research, great self-discipline, targets, and good goals. Establishing good trading plans is a clear reflection of great success in options trading.

Emotionally stable. Emotions can be quite a distraction as we get involved in different aspects of our lives. Losing a trade should be viewed just like a bad day that comes in handy with a good learning experience and knowledge for a bright future. Winning days should also be a learning day by valuing the good moves expressed that day.

Intensive learning and being proactive. Life always remains stagnant when you stop learning. Learning is achieved from the good side and the bad side, in that, master and learn every possible move expressed in options trading and be quite interested in picking the essence morals from the past episodes and squeezing any goodness from it. Also, subscribe to various well-contented channels and blogs to get the wide knowledge that is needed in options trading. Learning makes you informed and educated on the actual trade activities that are commonly involved in options trading.

Secure, accurate trading records. Try to learn from your mistakes though it can be tricky at times to formulate straight decisions based on your past performance since options trading is a matter of happy and sad seasons governed by several set strategies that have been correctly laid in the options trading plan. It is encouraged to learn from your past mistakes and get to grow strategically to become a successful options trader.

Determination and commitment. This entails the high thrust force that should govern a beginner or any kind of experienced trader to acquire what is best for him or her in options trading and getting to know the several tips on becoming a successful options trader.

Be flexible. Another point to add is that when you feel that the market does not suit you at all that particular options trading period, find something constructive to do. Master any possible market move that is likely to take place in options trading and master it.

Basic understanding and interpretation. The trader should familiarize himself or herself with the basic market terminologies to understand the basic activities of the market and get to know the various ways on how to begin and handle option trading. Interpretation involves getting to analyze the actual options trading happenings in the market and sourcing the essentials in every trading activity. This helps the trader to always look out for the reality of the market rather than the hype and depending on the major market deadlines.

Be aggressive. Being aggressive in options trading essentially implies that there is a thirst for great success, and the chances of acquiring large amounts of profits are so high. An aggressive option trader is mostly partaking in-depth research learning new and learning new lucrative trading moves. This gives the trader much experience and skills to face any kind of risks that are likely to be involved in the market and, within no time, the trader has accredited a great expert in options trading.

Emotionally stable. The trader involved in options trading should not be controlled by various feelings experienced in the market. The losing days should not discourage the trader in any way such that he or she decides to stick with the market hype. It is highly recommended that traders should follow their plan and always stick to their various strategies.

Good stock pick. An options trader needs to pick the right option to sell. Weigh whether you are capable of handling the respective stock and managing the necessary risks highly involved in it. Most importantly, is the stock going to benefit the trader from acquiring large amounts of profits?

Good capital management. Money is really important when it comes to trading. Monitor and plan for every amount of capital you plan to utilize in the market. Always be careful in the amount of money you place in every option. Acquiring losses is always an alternative when it comes to option trading, a breakdown that can tumble you so badly and make you bankrupt as well. Plan for the capital you plan to invest in the company.

Powerful trading platforms. The kind of platform where various trading activities are taking place is pretty much important in any kind of options trading involvement. Your best platform should consist of awesome navigation tools, learning sources, and other amazing features.

Selling options. Selling options is mostly preferred rather than buying options while practicing the call and put strategies that eventually help the trader to gain a good amount of profits.

Correct timing. As a trader, you should be informed of the good times and the bad times. Enter the market when the timing is quite favorable. Bad timing leads to great amounts of losses being made at the options trading market leading to a great downfall of finances. Bad timing leads to great amounts of losses being made at the options trading market leading to a great downfall of finances that, after all, causes bankruptcy.

Strategies to Be Successful in Options Trading

Good strategies set in the options trading plan should be prioritized. Back testing, measuring and weighing the current laid strategies by comparing them with some former historical records and learning the growth and the happenings that have happened in the recent periods, is highly recommended by the expert traders. Here are some strategies that should be considered:

Use a proper time period. A longer period, for instance, five years, is recommended during in-depth research and during analyzing the various sources to lay some good strategies. Remember to pick a quite long period to get the actual information and report in all that as part of learning.

Covered call. This kind of strategy involves both trading on the underlying stock and also to those of the options contract. The end goal of a covered call is to collect income through the premiums and majorly selling the stock amount that you already possess. Below are some the ways you need to consider in creating a covered call:

Purchase a stock and buy it in the form of shares.

For every 100 shares you own, sell a call contract.

Then hold on for the call to be exercised.

The kind of risk involved in covered calls holds the stock position carefully that could fail with time. The large chunks of profits of this particular call are equal to the price of a specific call option and a lower purchase price of the underlying stock.

Market put. This strategy involves the trader had made two purchases of stock trading and that of a put option. The benefit of this is that you, as an options trader, can shield oneself from several losses' occurrences. The market put is also considered advantageous during purchasing a security that is bearing a bullish outlook. The market put strategy is also essential when protecting depreciation in particular stock prices.

The market put is also referred to as a synthetic long call due to the similarities in the number of profit potentials on both sides.

Options spread. This strategy is established by selling several options and purchasing options of the same class and from the same security with various strike prices and expiration dates.

Butterfly spread. Butterfly involves four calls and puts and also considered as a market-neutral strategy that gets to pay most of its underlying stock without the concern of the expiration dates involved.

There are several varieties of butterfly spreads that normally use four kinds of options with three different strike prices. To add, different kinds of butterfly have different levels of the maximum profit amount and the maximum loss amount that are normally experienced during options trading.

Short bull ratio strategy. Short bull ratio strategy is used to benefit from the amounts of profits gained from increasing security involved in the trading market in a similar way in which we normally get to buy calls during a particular period.

CHAPTER 2 BEST STRATEGIES

Strategies make up a viable plan that is set to be used in any potential project.

What Type of Day Trading is Profitable?

What kind of day trading assets is much profitable? Below are some of the famous markets:

Foreign Exchange markets

Foreign Exchange markets are customarily carried out on the margin. I am trying to say that you can have more trades than what you have as a deposit. This could contribute to high profits on the business. Additionally, it depends on your day trading strategies and how you handle the risks in the business.

Stock markets

Stock markets are so popular that you buy and sell shares of a company.

Options markets

A trader in options trading can make a profit either by being a buyer or a seller. An options buyer can make a profit when the stock becomes higher or lower than the fixed price. In contrast, an options seller makes a profit when the asset settles above or under the fixed price.

Future markets

Future markets are also a right type of day trading. It depends on your experiences in trading. Also, to be profitable in this type of trading depends on the strategies you have employed in trading.

Rules to Be Successful in Day Trading

Strictly follow your trading plan

A disciplined life is sure of a successful life. After you have outlined your intended plan, be sure to be strict in following up. Being self-disciplined in your set target makes you ambitious, and chances of being successful in the future are high. A miss at your discipline is a great downfall; follow your desired motives step by step and erase the idea of getting rich quickly because it is a poisonous thought.

Learn every single day

Every person has a different way of learning. Make sure you set proper learning methods strategies.

Below are the most widely used methods of communication:

Videos

Videos are said to be popular because they are much practical. They outline the structural and visual learning about a particular topic and enhance much comprehension.

Blogs

Blogs have become a great source of information because they provide detailed and reliable sources of information. To identify the best blogs out, try goggling, and counter-check the blog's rates before you commence reading. Find the highly rated kinds of blogs and highly interactive depicted by the presence of a couple of comments.

Portable Document Format (PDF)

PDFs are easier to find one from the Internet and download it right away. They are pretty much available, reliable, and easy to go through and also make some modifications. There are different kinds of PDF with different kinds of information. Always double-check whatever you are reading. Remember to pick your PDF that goes hand in hand with your level of expertise.

Online learning has become a dominant kind of learning. You tube channel has become a favorite online learning channel for many people. The Internet is generally flooding with essential to advanced courses for like every field interested in this world. Look up to such educative videos. Explore the kind with a maximum number of views and discover the possibilities that are just about to unfold.

Remember to record (takedown) any viable information that happens to be so essential and outline the right steps expected to be established. This is the kind of strategy needed to produce large chunks of profits in the future.

Books

Books are made of pages.

Pages contain a page of any information concerning the topic in question. Okay, I am trying to justify that books contain quite a lot of information because of the number of its components. This implies that books are quite detailed and can be a good option for beginners because all they first need is quite some information.

Charts

Charts are reasonable graphical measures at day trading. They symbolize the progress and every activity taking place during day trading. They monitor and help examine the day trading events and aid to set up several possible likely to happen.

Do something irrelevant once in a while

Well, too much of something can indeed be poisonous. Take yourself out and do something different to enhance peace of mind and better future performances.

CHAPTER 3 DAY TRADING STRATEGIES

The ABCD Pattern

This is a harmonic pattern that is used to derive the other patterns of trade. This pattern is made up of three swings that are made up of the AB and CD lines, also known as the legs. The line BC is known as the correction line. The lines AB and CD are almost of the same size. The AB-CD pattern uses a downtrend that indicates that the reversal will be upward. On the other hand, the bearish pattern uses the uptrend than indicates there will be a reversal downward at some point. When using this pattern for trading, you must know the direction of the trend and the movement of the market. There are three types of ABCD pattern: the classic ABCD pattern, the AB=CD pattern, and the ABCD extension.

When using this pattern, remember that one can only enter the trade when the price has reached point D. Therefore, it is important to study the chart at the lows and highs; you can use the zigzag indicator, which marks the swings on the chart. As you study the chart, watch the price that forms AB and BC. In a bullish trade ABCD, C should be at the lower side of A.

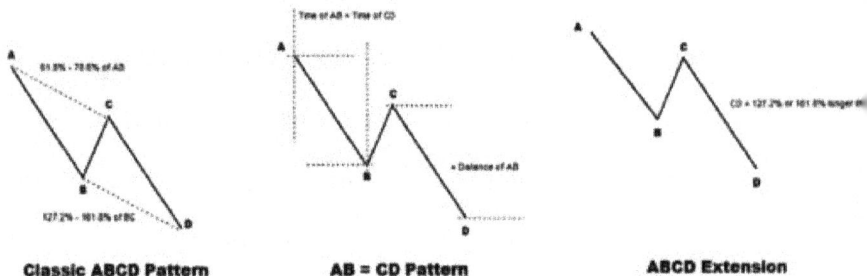

FIG1. ABCD Pattern

The point A, on the other hand, should be intermediate-high after B that is at a low point. D should be a new point that is lower than B. as mentioned earlier, the entry is at point D, but when the market reaches point D, you should not be too quick to enter the trade, consider other techniques that would make sure that the reverse is up when it is a bullish trade, and down when it is a bearish trade.

Flag Momentum

In a trading market, there are times when things are good and the traders enjoy an upward trend, which gives a chart pattern that represents a bull flag pattern. It is named as such because when you look at the chart, it forms a pattern that resembles a flag on a pole. The trend in the market is an uptrend, and therefore the pattern is referred to as a bullish flag. The bull flag pattern is characterized by the following; when the stock makes a positive move with a relatively high volume, the pole is formed, when the stock consolidates on a lighter volume at the top, the flag is formed. The stock continues to move at a relatively high volume breaking through the consolidation pattern. The bull flag momentum is a trading strategy that can be used at any given time frame. When it is used to scalp the movements of price, the bull is used only on two instances of time frame: the second and the fifth minute time frames. The trading bull flags also work well when using daily charts to trade and can also be used effectively when swing trading. It is simple to trade, but it is challenging to look for the exact bull pattern. This problem can be solved using scanners that help to look for stocks on the upward trend and wait for them to be in a consolidation position at the top. The best and free scanners that can be used to locate bull flags are Fenves and Chart Mill. There are tips that can be used to indicate a bull flag. When there is an increase in stock volume that is influenced by news, and when the stock prices remain high, showing a clear pattern for a pullback. At this point, you can now check out when the prices break out above the consolidation pattern or on high volumes of stock. To make a move, place a stop order at the bottom of the consolidation. At this point, the ratio of risk to reward is 2:1, and it is the best time to target. The strongest part of the pattern is the volume of the stock, and it is a good sign that there will be a major move and a successful breakout. On the trend, it is also good to look at the descending trend as it gives a sign on the next breakout. This can be seen in the trend line that is found on at the topmost of the flag.

When used well for trading, the bull flags are effective tools of the trade, however, things can go wrong, and therefore one must be ready with an exit strategy. There are two strategies, one is placing a stop order at a point below the consolidation area, and the second method is using a moving average that is monitored for within 20 days. Within the 20 days, if the price of the stock is below the moving average, then it is time to close out the position and try out other trading routes.

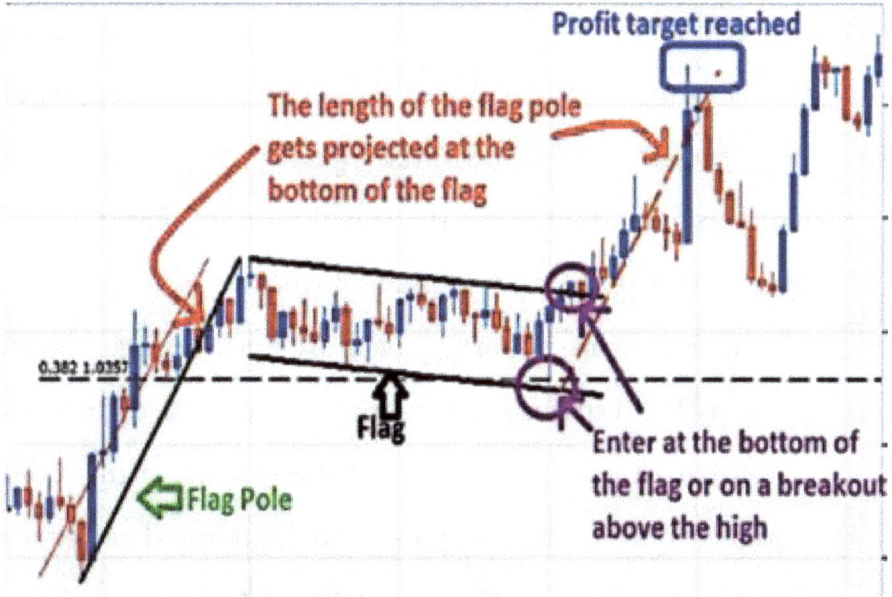

FIG2. Flag Momentum

Reversal Trading

Reversal trading, also known as a trend reversal pattern, is a trading strategy that indicates the end of a trend and the start of a new one. This pattern is formed when the price level of stock in the current trend has reached a maximum. This pattern provides information on the possible change of trend and possible value of price movement. A pattern that is formed in the upwards trend signals that there would be a reversal in the trend and the prices will go down soon. Conversely, a downward trend will indicate that there will be a movement of the prices and it will be upwards. For you to recognize this pattern, you must know where specific patterns form in the current trend. There are distribution patterns that occur at the top of the market; at this point, traders sell more than they buy. The patterns that occur at the bottom of the markets are referred to as accumulation patterns, and at this point, traders buy more than they sell.

Reversal trends are formed at all time frames, and it is because the bank traders have either place trades are taking profits off the trades. The trend can be detected when there are multiple up and down formations that are fully formed;

they should be at least two upswings and two downswings indicating a bearish pattern.

The swing highs of lows on the trend line depend on which reversal pattern is formed. The highs or lows form at a similar price because the bank traders want to appear as if they are causing a reversal in the market, by getting all their trades places at the same time. In the real sense, that is not the case because they appear at different points of the trend. Therefore, as a trader, you should wait for a clear and steady trend upward for you to sell in the case of a bullish trade and a steady trend downward for the case of a bearish trade for you to buy.

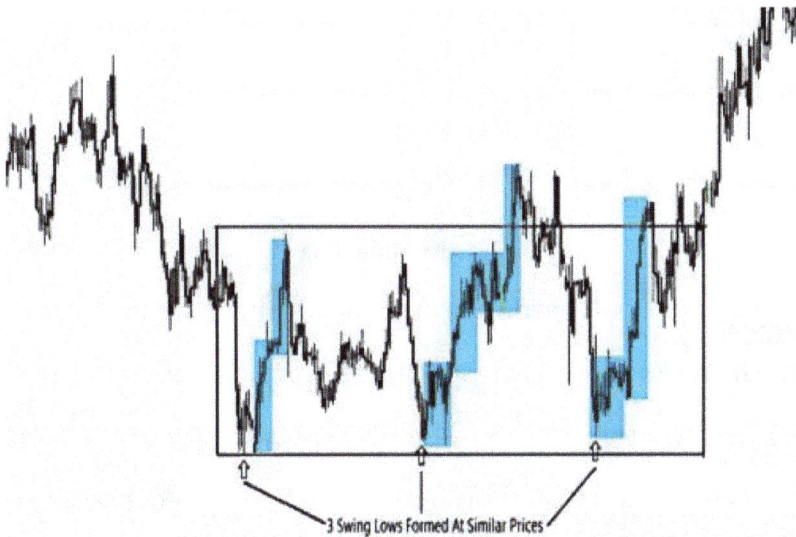

3 Swing Lows Formed At Similar Prices

FIG3. Reversal trading

There are different types of reversal patterns. The double top reversal pattern is a pattern that has two tops on the chart. It looks like "M." The double top has its reverse type known as the double bottom pattern that resembles "W." The double bottom has two bottoms located either on the same support or at different supports.

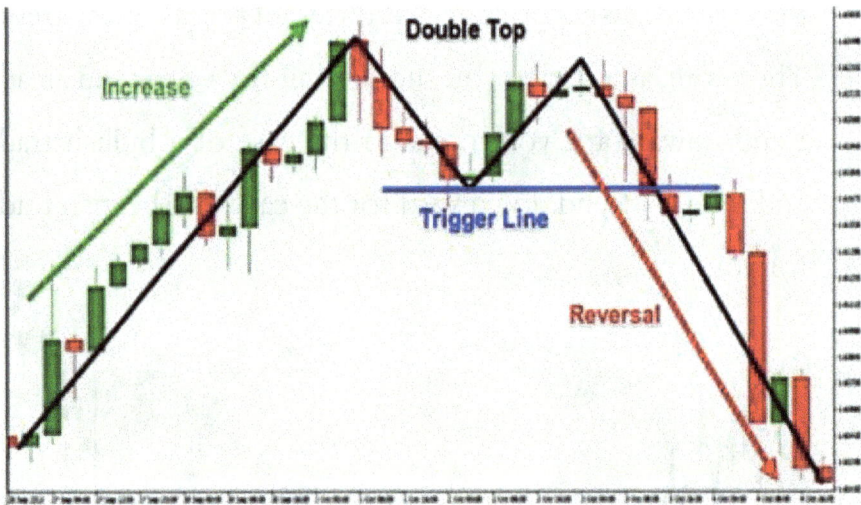

Double Top

Increase

Trigger Line

Reversal

FIG4. Double Top

Another reversal pattern is the head and shoulders; this pattern resembled two shoulders and ahead. The two shoulders are tops that are slightly below the other top that is known as the head. The head and shoulders can also be represented in a descending pattern whereby the tops become bottoms.

Moving Average Trend Trading

This strategy of trading is common among traders and it uses technical indicators. A moving average helps to know which way the price is moving, if the moving average is inclined upwards, then the price is moving up, and if it is inclined downwards, then the price is going downwards. Moving average can also help to show resistance or support of the trend, but this depends on the amount of time of the moving average. Support is shown when the trend of the price is downward, and at this point, the selling pressure reduces, and buyers start to step in the market. Resistance is shown when the trend in the price of the stock is upward. At this point, buying of stock reduces and sellers step in. It should be noted that the prices of trade stock do not always follow the moving average, but it is good to know that when the stock price is above the moving average of the trend, then the price trend is upward. Conversely, if the price is below the moving average, then the trend of the price of the stock is downwards.

Moving average is a powerful tool of the trade as it is easy to calculate, which makes it popular among traders. This tool of trade enables the trader to understand the current trend and identify any signs of a reversal. It also helps the trader to determine entry into the trade or an exit, depending on whether it offers support or resistance.

There are different types of moving averages. The simple moving average, which sums up five recent closing prices and calculates the average price, another one is the exponential moving average, whose calculation is a bit complex because it applies more weighting to the data that is most recent. When the simple moving average and the exponential moving averages are compared, the exponential moving average is affected more by the changes in prices that the simple moving average.

FIG5. Moving Average

VWAP Trading

VWAP is the volume-weighted average price. It is a trading strategy that is simple and highly effective when you are trading in a short time frame. For it to work for you, you must use different strategies, and the most common strategy is the waiting for a VWAP cross above and enter long. A VWAP that is across above gives signals to the traders that buyers would be entering the market, and there would be an upward movement of price. The bearish traders might short stock giving it a VWAP cross below, thus signaling the buyers to leave the market and take profits. VWAP can also be used as a resistance or support level for determining the risk of a trade. When the stock trades above the VWAP, the VWAP is used as the support level, and when the trading is below the VWAP, the VWAP is used as a resistance level. In both cases, the trader is guided by the VWAP to know when to buy and when to sell. When doing trading transactions, trading costs are determined by comparing the price of the transaction, against a reference or a benchmark, and the most common benchmark is the VWAP. The daily VWAP benchmark encourages traders to avoid risks of trading on extreme prices of the day by spreading their trades over time. This trading strategy favors those people who use market orders to trade rather than limit orders. This is because an opportunity cost arises from delays and passive trading.

CHAPTER 4 SWING TRADING STRATEGIES

Regularly Scanning for Trades

Fenves provides you with a wealth of information as well as allowing you to scan for stocks that meet your own defined parameters. You do not need the subscription version of these websites unless you plan on doing more sophisticated scans and back testing. Back testing is the process of trying out a trading strategy on historical data. This helps you to confirm that the strategy you have developed has a good chance of success before you put your actual capital at risk. I am confident though that the free Fenves or Chart Mill website service will meet most of your needs. Let's look at the Fenves site specifically and see how it can be used to scan for and find trading opportunities. Chart Mill works in a comparable fashion and, if you choose to instead use your broker's site, then you will likely go through a similar process as follows:

1) review overall market conditions

2) review the performance of market sectors

3) screen for opportunities

4) review the short list of opportunities

Let's go through each step in the process as outlined above.

Review Overall Market Conditions

When you open up the Fenves home page you will see an overwhelming amount of information – let's keep it simple and look at what I feel are the most important pieces of data. You will see 3 bar charts at the top of the page that show the DOW, Nasdaq, and S&P performances for the day. However, as a swing trader, you should be more interested in the data just under those charts, which includes:

- % advancing versus declining (stocks up on the day versus down)
- % new highs versus new lows
- % stocks above their 50-day SMA and % below
- % stocks above their 200-day SMA and % below
- % bull-bear sentiment of subscribers

All of these indicators tell you much about the direction of the market and the sentiment of traders. These are often referred to as internal indicators for the overall market.

Much like paddling a boat in a river, it is easier to paddle downstream with the river's current versus paddling into the current. Strong paddlers may make headway upriver, but the average and poor paddlers are going to be swept downstream no matter which direction they are paddling. It is the same with securities; there will always be some securities in a strong trend that will defy the market and go in the opposite direction, while the majority of securities will move with the overall market. In markets that are trending very strongly in one direction, almost all of the stocks will be swept in the direction of the current.

In a market that is trending strongly in one direction, swing traders should be more inclined to find trades that are moving in the same direction as the overall market. For example, if you see these indicators showing many more stocks are declining versus advancing, and the percentage of new lows are much higher than new highs, and a greater percentage of stocks are dropping under their 50 and 200-day SMAs, then we are in a strong down-trending market.

The size of that downtrend will be reflected in the actual numbers for each of these measures. If stocks making new lows are at 80% compared to only 20% making new highs, then it indicates a strong bear market overall and swing traders should be looking at short opportunities more than long trades. Figure below shows these indicators on the Fenves site.

When this image was taken the market was not strongly trending one way or the other and most of the indicators were sitting in the middle of their ranges. For example, the new highs compared to new lows were 123 versus 107 respectively, which is slightly bullish but not considered a strong up trending market.

FIG6. Fenves website - the overall market indicators.

In summary, it is beneficial to be informed on how the market is performing so you can consider aligning your trades in the same direction.

Review Performance of Market Sectors

Taking this alignment concept, a little further, a swing trader will also be concerned with the various sectors in the market and how they are performing. You will hear professional traders and analysts talk about "rotation" in the market or how a particular sector is leading the market higher. This means that traders and investors are moving capital from one sector to another or they are favoring certain sectors over other ones. Fenves offers a very good tool to determine which sectors are performing well and which are performing poorly over several different time frames. By selecting the Groups tab on the home page, you will see some bar charts that show performance by sector for 1-day, 1-week, 1, 3 and 6-month periods. This illustration provides a quick and easy way to survey the specific sectors in the market to see which one's investors and traders currently favor and which ones are out of favor.

Figure below shows an image of the page taken at the end of April 2018. At the time this screenshot was taken, it was the utility and health care sector stocks that were showing strength over the previous 1-week and 1-month time frame.

Over the previous month, basic materials had done well, but their weekly performance indicated that this sector had now slipped lower.

A screenshot of the Fenves Groups tab showing which sectors are in favor and which are out of favor over multiple time frames.

While it will not show in the print edition of this book, you will see on the Fenves website that the sectors which are out of favor (the bottom rows in each time frame) appear in brighter shades of red depending upon how out of favor they are. Likewise, the more in favor a sector is (the top rows in each time frame), the brighter the shade of green they are presented in (in the black and white figure are the first lines of each sector in light gray). Long and short opportunities, you should take note of the sectors at the top of the charts and which ones are at the bottom.

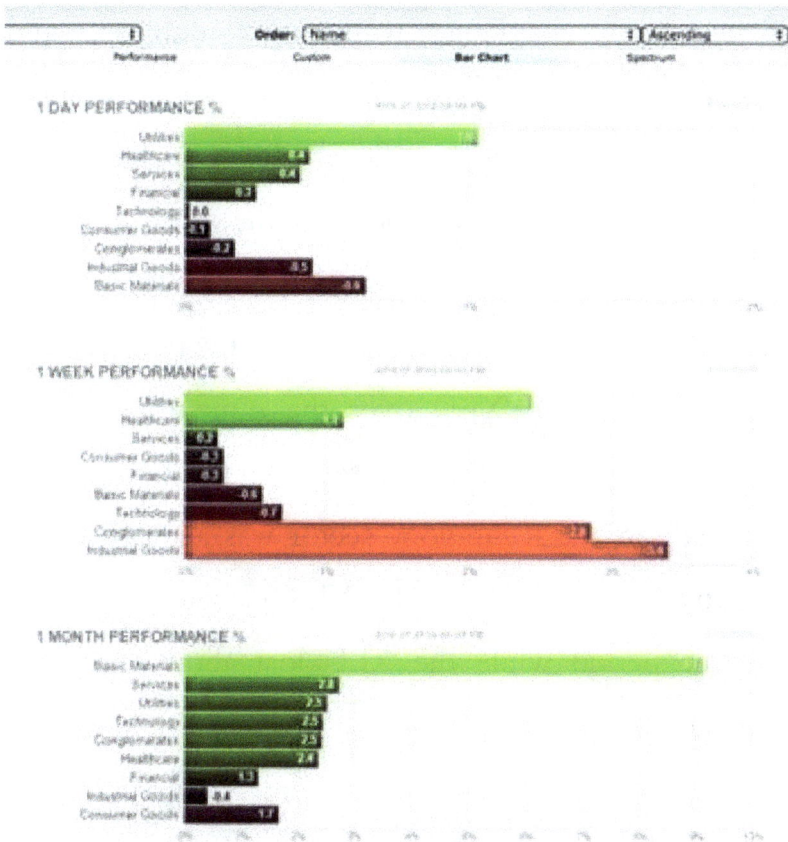

FIG7. A Screenshot Fenves Group tab - Sectors

In addition, look for the alignment of multiple time frames: for example, is the 1-week and 1-month performance of a sector aligned? Don't forget that I suggested it is better to have an alignment of your swing trades on several timelines and not just one. Being aligned in a sector can be even more beneficial compared to being only aligned with the market. Consider that the market is made up of different sectors such as retail, banking, technology, defense, and transportation to name but a few. While some of these sectors could be making significant moves higher, other sectors may be performing poorly at the same time. To illustrate this point, let's look at the performance of the XLK Technology ETF and compare it to the performance of the Utilities ETF XLU over the same time frame. Referring to Figure 12.3, you can see from the 2 charts that a long trade in the technology sector was a much better trade compared to utilities. The XLK gained about 10% during the period while the XLU lost about the same percentage.

FIG8. Compare the performance XLU vs XLK

Charts comparing the performance over the same period of 2 ETFs, the XLU versus the XLK.

In summary, if you are considering an individual stock, check the sector category it is in to see how the overall sector is performing. Are you trading with an overall sector trend or against it? You should also check multiple timelines to make sure that they are aligned or at least showing signs of reversing. If you do not get confirmation that the longer-term sector trend is moving or starting to move in your expected direction, then you might just be trading a short-term correction that will turn against you. This will ensure that you are on the right side of a trend or trend change and not just looking at a short-term correction. The next step is to start to look for specific trading opportunities.

Screen for Opportunities

In the next step of the scanning process on the Fenves site, you will select the Screener Tab. Figure 12.4 shows what this page will look like when selected. Near the top, you will see 3 tabs called Descriptive, Technical and Fundamental. By working with these 3 tabs, you can filter out stocks that meet specific parameters. With no filters in place, the total number of stocks listed on this page is an overwhelming 7,438 at the time of writing.

CHAPTER 5 LONG TERM TRADING STRATEGIES

You can start trading with these low risk strategies today. I will provide you with the tools and techniques to implement these strategies so that you can increase your account size and build a strong base of knowledge on how trading works. The strategies are suitable for both long and short term trading; from intraday scalping up to day trading or swing-trading.

In today's volatile markets, you should not take big risks with your trading capital. You should focus on following a well-defined and tested system. More importantly, a system that provides superior profits in the long term with low drawdowns in the trading account. The best way to achieve this is by using the Price Action Techniques to capture these price reversals as they happen.

These techniques are easy to learn and implement, but it takes many hours of hard work to master them effectively.

I will provide you with the trading and risk management rules to follow.

The price action techniques are equally suitable for all time frames, from intraday scalping up to day trading or swing-trading.

This is the Trading Strategy I have been using to trade Forex, Futures & Shares for my own account and I would like to share it with you. You are welcome to join me in this journey. As you know, sharing is very important in trading, especially with the same goals and objectives.

This is an Intraday trading strategy with high risk profile. It provides a big opportunity to earn high returns as the market swings in a favourable direction, but it comes with higher risk. The key purpose of this intraday trading strategy is to capture price reversals and use Fibonacci retracements to buy more or sell short depending on what the market condition is like.

The key purpose of this Trade is to capture price reversals and use Fibonacci retracements to buy more or sell short depending on what the market condition is like. Let's say you bought a stock at $10 and it goes up quickly to $15, then you have missed a golden opportunity to sell the stock at $15 and take profit. Conversely, if you sold your stock at $10 and takes profit. If you bought the stock at $10 and the price falls to $5, then you have missed a golden opportunity to buy more shares at $5 and sell at $15.

The Entry Rule:

Buy a stock when market price is above the 200-day moving average line. Exit position once the market price comeback and retrace below the same moving average line again. Sell a stock when market price is below its moving average line. Exit position once the market price comeback and retrace above this moving average line again.

The Exit Rule:

Exit a stock immediately when it retraces below the 200-day moving average line. The Exit move should be no more than 50% of the initial buy entry price, otherwise the trade is considered as a "No Participate" trade and trading risk is high. Exit when it retraces 50% of the initial entry price. Sell at market price when above its moving average line. Exit position once the market price comeback and retrace above this moving average line again.

The Entry and Exit price levels are important as it represents the valid buy and sell levels that are not far from the current price. The trade is valid as long as the entry and exit prices are not breached.

If the entry price is breached, then your stop loss should be placed below your buy entry level, otherwise you will lose money if there is a large move in a negative direction.

If the exit price is breached, then your stop loss should be placed above your sell exit level, otherwise you will lose money if there is a large move in a negative direction.

The trade takes place at market price when above its moving average line. If the share price is below this moving average line and it reverses higher with strong volume, then it's considered as an entry and that stock is bought. The same entry signal on the other side of the moving average line indicates that the shares are sold.

CHAPTER 6 OPTIONS STRATEGIES

Long Straddle

In a long straddle, you'll simultaneously buy a put and call for the same underlying stock. You're also going to want the same strike price and expiration date. This technique is something that can be utilized with a highly volatile stock. That way you have the possibility of profiting no matter which way the stock moves. Before we see how this works, let's step back for a second and recall how we determine whether or not a deal is going to be profitable. We are looking at this from the buyer's perspective.

In a call option, you're going to profit when the stock exceeds the strike price. However, you must remember to include the premium in your calculation. If you think a stock will go higher than $54, but you're paying a $1 premium per share, then you will have to invest in a call option that has a strike price of at least $55.

In a put option, it's the same game, but you're hoping the stock will go below the strike price. So, for our new scenario of buying a call and a put at the same strike price and expiration date, we will buy a put with a strike price of $55. For simplicity, we will stay with a $1 premium.

Now you need to know the net premium, which will be the sum of the premium from the call option + the premium from the put option, in this case, $2.

You can get a profit when one of two conditions are met:

- Price of underlying stock > (Strike price of call + Net Premium). In our example, you will make a profit when the amount of the underlying stock is higher than $55 + $2 = $57.

- Price of underlying stock < (Strike price of put – Net Premium). Using our example, you'll see a profit when the price of the underlying stock is less than $55- $2 = $53.

The maximum loss for a straddle will occur when the contract expires with the underlying trading at the strike price. In that case, both contracts expire, and you're out the premiums paid for both options.

A long straddle has two break-even points. These are:

- Lower breakeven point: Strike price – Net premium
- Upper breakeven point: Strike price + Net premium

Remember you buy both options with the same strike price and expiration date.

Let's look at a simple example. A stock is trading at $100 a share in May. The investor buys a call with a strike price of $200 that expires on the third Friday in June for $100. The investor also buys a put with a strike price of $200 that expires on the third Friday of June for $100.

The net premium is $100 + $100 = $200.

Now suppose that on the expiry date, the stock is trading at $300. The put expires as worthless since the stock price of the underlying is far above the strike price of the put. However, the investor's call option expires in the money with an intrinsic value of 100 x ($300 - $200) = $10,000. Less the premium the investor has made $9,800.

On the other hand, suppose that the stock drops in value, and on the expiry is trading at $50. This time, the call option expires as worthless. The investor can buy 100 shares at a price of $50 each for a total cost of $5,000. Now he can sell them to exercise the put option at $200 a share, so he nets $20,000 - $5,000 - $200 = $14,800.

This is a fictitious example, so whether the numbers are realistic or not really isn't the point – the point is that the investor will profit no matter what happens to the stock price.

Strangle

The term strangle is an adaptation of the straddle. In this case, you also simultaneously buy a call option and a put option. However, instead of buying them at the same strike price, you buy them at different strike prices. For this type of strategy, you will buy slightly out-of-money options. This is used when you think that the underlying stock will undergo significant volatility in the short term. You will achieve a profit with a strangle when one of two conditions are met:

- Price of underlying stock > (strike price of call + Net Premium paid) or

Price of underlying stock < (strike price of put − Net premium paid)

Usually, the strike price of the put is set at a lower value. Profit is determined by one of two possibilities:

- Profit = Price of underlying stock − strike price of call − net premium

- Profit = Strike price of put– the price of underlying stock – net premium

Bear Spread

A bear spread is profitable when the underlying stock price declines. Like the above strategies, a bear spread involves the simultaneous purchase of more than one option; however, in a bear spread, you buy two options of the same type. Alternatively, a call bear spread involves selling a call with a low strike price and buying a call with a high strike price.

Bull Spread

A bull spread is designed to profit when the price of the underlying security has a modest price increase. You can do a bull spread using either call or put options.

Married Puts

A married put is basically an insurance policy like that we described earlier. You buy a stock and a put option at the same time, in order to protect yourself against possible losses from the stock.

Cash Secured Puts

In a cash-secured put, you secure the possible purchase of stock by having money in your brokerage account to cover the purchase. This will allow you to purchase stock at a discount, provided you have enough money in your account to actually buy the stock. In short, you write a put option and set aside the cash to purchase the stock. Cash secured put is done when you are bullish on the underlying stock but believe it will undergo a temporary downturn.

Rolling

Rolling a trade simply means that you are simultaneously closing out your existing positions and opening new ones based on the same underlying stock. When rolling a position, you can change the strike price, the duration of the contract, or both. You can roll forward, which means to extend the expiration date for the option.

A roll-up means that you increase the strike price when you open the new contract. A roll-up is used on a call option when you believe the underlying stock is going to increase in price. When you are trading put options, you use a roll down. In that case, you close your option and reopen it with the same underlying stock but with a lower strike price. A higher strike price means that the new position will be cheaper. When rolling, you're going out in time to deadline. When rolling a call, you're hoping that the stock will rise in price. In this case, you're rolling to an out of the money position. The price of the new call will drop. With a put, the opposite occurs, and the price of the new put will increase.

CHAPTER 7   PRACTICAL
EXAMPLES AND
STRATEGIES

If you set up with a dealer, and you have got your very own trading room ready to go, a successful plan would be needed. Day-trading techniques come in all shapes and sizes, some simple and others complex. Before we look at an example, there are a few critical components that will involve most techniques. When you transact using the internet, you can typically use charts and trends to forecast potential changes in prices. They are based on fundamental theory, that history is repeating itself, and you will find many a wealthy trader who wholeheartedly agrees with that assertion.

Your map will claim the latest selling options indicators. These vary from strategy to strategy, which includes the Put-Call Ratio Tracker Capital Flow Index Open Interest Relative Strength Index Bollinger Bands. You will find that it takes hard work and experience to exchange trends for options. You would need to smooth out any creases and try several different charts before you find one with numbers that paints a good picture.

Covered Call Options

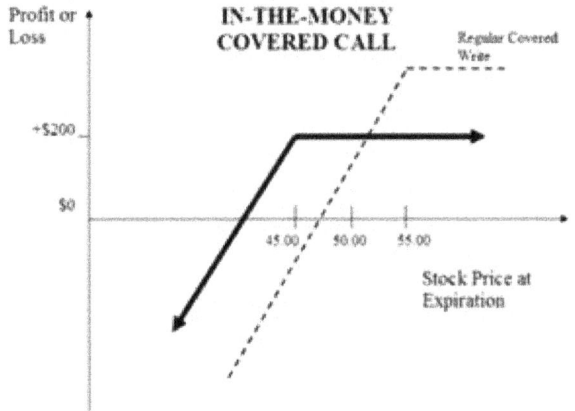

Profit or Loss / IN-THE-MONEY COVERED CALL / Regular Covered Write / +$200 / $0 / 45.00 50.00 55.00 / Stock Price at Expiration

A call option is a contract option in which the holder (buyer) has the right (but not the obligation) to purchase a defined volume of a commodity at a predetermined date (strike price) within a given time (until its expiry).

This constitutes a duty for the writer (seller) of a call option to sell the underlying security at strike price if the option is exercised. A prime is paid to the call choice writer for taking on the risk involved with the responsibility.

Each deal includes 100 shares, with stock options. The short call is protected if the writer of the call option owns the required amount of the security underlying it. The covered call is a common option technique that helps the stockholder to produce additional income from their stock holdings by periodic call options sales. Someone should buy a bull call spread as an alternative to writing covered calls with a comparable benefit opportunity but with considerably less capital need. Instead of buying the underlying shares of the covered call strategy, the preferred bull call spread approach requires only that the trader purchase deep-in-the-money call options.

Because the aim of writing protected calls is to collect premiums, it makes sense to sell near-month options when time decay on those options is at its highest. Hence, the two tactics we equate would include selling marginally out-of-the-money call options in the near-month timeframe.

Married Put Options

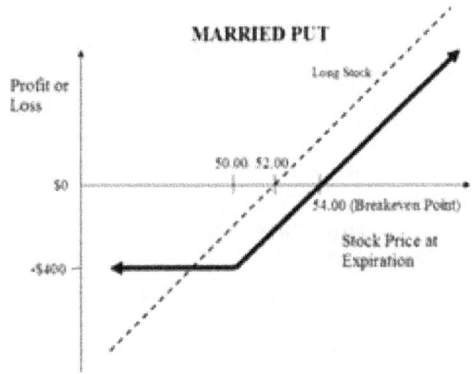

Both married put and long call have the same infinite benefit potential with no cap onto the underlying stock price appreciation. However, benefit is often lower than just owning the stock, lowered by the cost or premium of the purchased option. Reaching break-even for strategy happens when the underlying stock increases by the number of premium options received. Anything beyond that is income.

The advantage of a married put is that the stock now has a floor minimizing downside risk. The floor is the difference between the underlying stock price, when the put was bought, and the put strike price. Simply put, when the option was acquired, if the underlying stock sold precisely at the strike price, the strategy loss is capped at exactly the price paid for the opportunity.

A married put is also called a long synthetic call, as it has the same profile. The strategy resembles purchasing a standard call option (without the underlying stock) because for both, the same dynamic is real: limited risk, infinite profit potential. The difference between these approaches is clearly how much less money a long call takes.

Bull Call Spread Options

One may buy a bull call spread as an alternative to writing covered calls with a comparable benefit opportunity but

Profit or Loss

BULL CALL SPREAD

$300

40.00   45.00

$0

42.00   Stock Price at Expiration

-$200

with considerably less capital need. Because of purchasing the underlying stock of the covered call strategy, the preferred bull call spread approach requires only that the trader buy deep-in-the-money call options.

If the aim of writing protected calls is to collect premiums, it makes sense to sell near month options when time decay for those options is at its highest. Hence, the two tactics we equate would include selling marginally out-of-the-money call options in the near-month period. The distribution of the bull call reduces the call option's risk, but it comes at a trade-off. The stock market returns are also capped, thereby having a small spectrum where the buyer will make a return. Traders will use the spread of the bull call as they expect the valuation of a commodity should increase moderately. Quite likely, they will use this technique at periods of high uncertainty.

The distribution of the bull call consists of steps which require two call options.

Pick the investments that you believe would grow over a given span of days, weeks, or months. Buy a call option on a particular closing date at a strike price above the selling rate and pay the premium. With this alternative, another name is a long call. Around the same time, sell a call option at a higher strike price and has the same expiry date as the first call option. Another term for a quick call for this alternative is.

Bear Put Spread Options

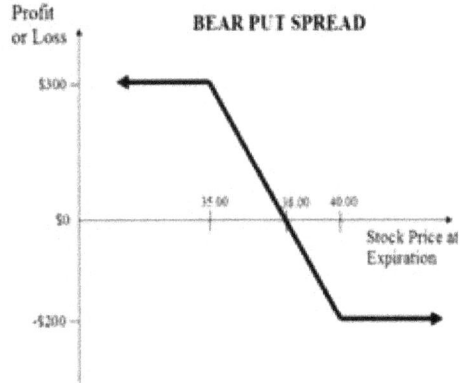

A bear put spread is a form of options strategy where an investor or trader expects a moderate downturn in security or asset prices. Bear put propagation is accomplished by purchasing put options when selling the same number of puts on the same security at the same expiry date at a lower strike price. With this method, the potential profit is the difference between the two strike costs, minus the options' net value.

For a note, an option is a right to sell a given quantity of underlying security at a defined strike price.

Often known as a debit put spread or a long-put spread. A bear put spread is an options technique executed by a bearish trader who aims to increase income while reducing profits.

A bear put spread approach entails purchasing and selling puts on the same underlying asset at the same expiry date but at different strike rates.

A bear puts spread net profit as the price of the underlying security decreases. Therefore, net capital outlay is smaller than buying a single put outright. It also carries much less risk than shortening stock or protection, as the risk is limited to bear put spread net expense. Theoretically, selling a stock short has infinite chance if price goes higher. Unless the investor assumes the underlying stock or asset would decline by a small sum between the day of settlement and the expiry date, a bear put spread may be a perfect strategy. But, if the underlying stock or security declines by more than the dealer gives up the right to demand the extra Benefit. The trade-off between risk and future gain draws many traders.

Protective Collar Options

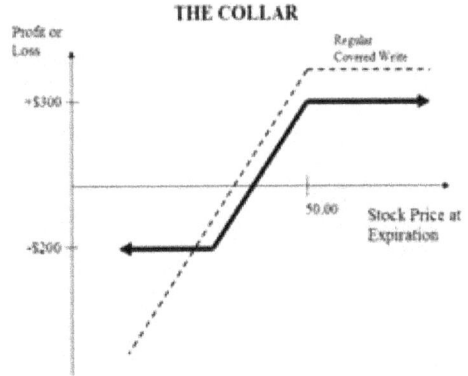

THE COLLAR

The protective collar technique is where you purchase some protection options, sell a short call option, and purchase a long-placed option to reduce downside risk. This technique defends stocks from low market values. It uses cash-on-call options when sold and a Put option when purchased.

Everyone else holds short securities, and the lender must pay the responsibility. Long Put Option is purchasing shares, assuming the stock price should be smaller than the expiry strike price. The investor holds the shares.

Fast call option – selling the current call option until the investor feels market price would sink below the call strike point. The holder will benefit. Although the buyer will not own these shares, they must purchase them again later as the price falls and pay the owner.

Long and Short Strangle Options

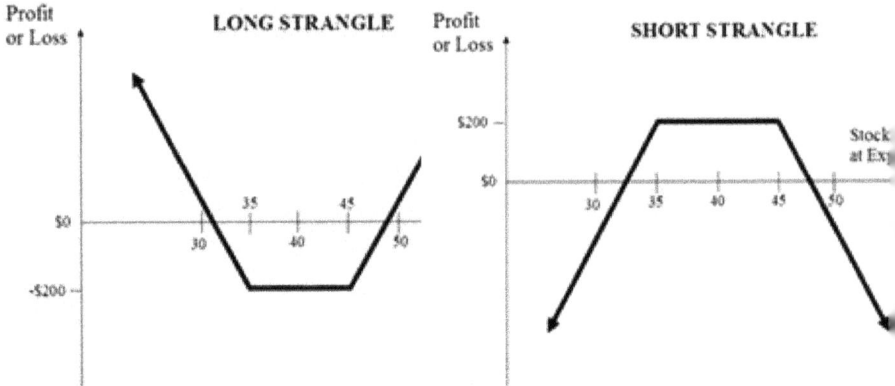

The endless options strangle a tremendous benefit, minimal risk approach that is taken while the dealer of the options considers the underlying stock and expiry date. Significant returns are obtained with the long strangle option strategy when the underlying stock price takes a very considerable step either upward or downward at expiry. The formula for estimating profit is given below:

Maximum Benefit = Unlimited Benefit Gained When Underlying Price > Long Call Strike Price + Net Premium Paid OR Underlying Price < Long Put Strike Price — Net Premium Paid Income = Underlying Price — Long Call Strike Price — Net Premium Paid OR Long Put Strike Price — Underlying Price — Net Premium Paid

A medium strangles one quick call with a higher trigger price and one low shot. All options have the same underlying supply and expiry date but different strike rates. If the underlying stock trades in a narrow range below the break-even points, a short strangle is formed for a net credit (or net receipt). Benefit opportunity is limited to cumulative contributions earning fewer commissions. Potential liability is infinite if stock demand increases, and asset selling declines significantly. Full benefit efficiency is limited to overall fewer commissions earned. Total Benefit is gained if the short strangle expires, the stock price trades at or below strike rates, and all options expire worthlessly. The maximum probability of profit loss is infinite because the stock price can grow forever. The potential risk is significant on the downside when the stock price can fall to zero.

CHAPTER 8 ADVANCED STRATEGIES FOR OPTION TRADING

Options Strategies

It specifies what you wish to do with your options and how long you want to trade in them. You must also know how much you are looking at making so that you can dispose of your options as soon as you reach your end goal. A strategic plan will be a tool that you can use to know about the resources that are at your disposal and how well you plan on using them. They will help you achieve whatever you wish to from the markets while cutting down on loss potential.

Trading strategies can help people get what they want from their trades and why they are trading in the first place. It helps in outlining the various steps that are involved in evaluating, executing and taking care of your options portfolio. Before you get started with it, there happen to be a few things that you need to know or develop before initiating the trade.

One thing to understand is that just because you have a good strategy in place does not mean that it will always work out in your favor. You might run into some issues and end up losing a little on your profit. You have to be prepared for it and have a few plans in place that will help you offset it.

It might be quite simple to develop a strategy that is unique to you. All you have to do is spend some time thinking about the strategy that will work for an investor of your caliber. Remember that no one strategy will work for all, and it is all about finding your path. To help you come up with some of these strategies, these will highlight some tips for you. Before that, let us look at the benefits of strategic planning.

- There is a vast difference in making plans in advance and acting impulsively. If you have plans in place, then you will be able to take the right steps when there is a need to do so. In short, strategic planning can help you invest the money that is at your disposal and make the most of it. You, therefore, have to be proactive and not reactive.

- You must have a plan of action and ensure that you attain the goals that you set out to achieve. If you keep waiting for things to fall into place, then it will not work out and take forever for it to happen. But if you take action now, then you will be able to capitalize on the opportunity and ensure that you set up an ideal market for yourself. You do not have to be scared of the market, pulling up a sneaky one and be prepared for all the things that might come your way.

- A strategic plan will guide you and prepare you for any emergencies. As you know, it is impossible to understand how markets can operate, and it is vital to be ready for whatever comes your way. If you make the effort of putting a plan in place, then it will work in your favor. You can have a sense of direction and know exactly which way the markets will move and whether you are prepared for it.

- The key is to understand that there will be many scenarios in the market, and it will be impossible to know which way things will move. You have to have a clear understanding of what you wish to achieve and why you want it. These might sound too basic, but it is essential to answer these questions if you're going to make the most of your options trading strategies. You should know exactly how much you will be investing and where. It can leverage your earnings and make sure you make much higher.

- It is only through consistent patience that you will be able to attain your end goals.

Covered Call

Also known as a buy-write, this describes the act of selling the right to purchase a specified asset that you own at a specified price within a specified amount of time, which is usually less than 12 months. It is a two-part strategy whereby someone first purchases stock then sells it on the share-by-share prices.

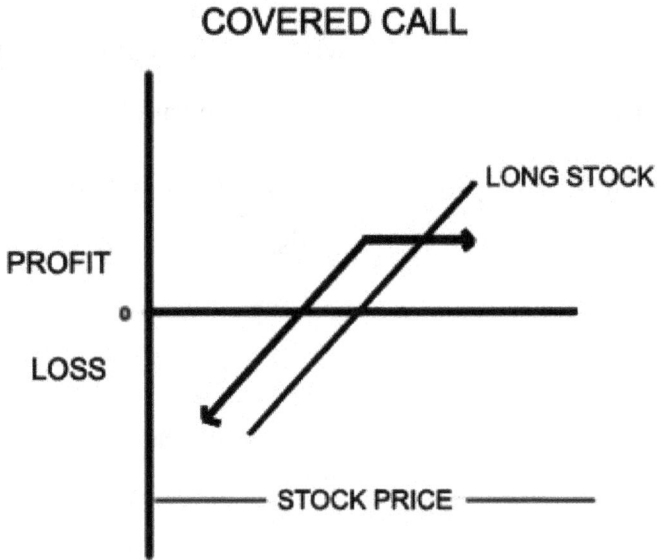

COVERED CALL

LONG STOCK

PROFIT

0

LOSS

STOCK PRICE

The beauty of this type of option is that the seller benefits by receiving a premium payment from the holder of the options. Risk is mitigated because the seller already owns the stock. Therefore, your costs are covered if the stock price rises above the strike price. If the trader chooses to exercise the right to purchase on or before the expiration date, you simply deliver as agreed and rip any additional benefits.

Stock is the most common asset used in this type of option.

If you choose to consider covered calls, at your price, you need to be willing to own the stock, and it is even if the price depreciates. Remember that there is no guarantee that you will earn significantly on the stock that you have purchased due to the volatility of financial markets. Therefore, you need to be diligent in your focus on seeking good quality stocks that you are willing to own. You need to be able to still potentially benefit from that ownership if there are down periods in the market.

As the seller of a covered call option, you need to be also willing to part with that stock if the price rises. You cannot change your mind if the price of the stock goes up if you have already entered into an option with a willing buyer. You must exercise that delivery if the trader chooses to use that option.

The maximum potential profit of covered calls will be achieved if the stock price is met at or above the strike price of that call at or by the expiration date. The formula for this is as follows:

Sum of the Call Premium + (Strike Price - Stock Price) = Maximum Potential Profit

The seller also needs to consider the break-even point at the expiration date. The formula for this is as follows:

Purchase Price of the Stock - The Call Premium = Break-Even Analysis

The seller also needs to determine the maximum risk potential. It is equal to the purchasing price of the stock at the break-even point.

The seller also needs to be satisfied with the static rate of return and the if-called rate of return on the stocks. The static performance is the approximate annual net profit of a covered call, assuming that the stock price does not change until the expiration date and until the option expires. To calculate this value, the seller needs to know:

- The purchase price of the particular stock

- The price of the option (strike)

- The price of the call

- The number of days until option expires

- If there are any dividends and the amount of these dividends

Calculating these factors leads to a percentile figure being determined. The formula for calculating this is:

(Call + Dividend) / Stock Price × Time Factor = Static Rate of Return

The if-called return is an approximate annual net profit on a covered call with the assumption that the stock price is above the strike price by or on the expiration of the option and that the stock is sold at termination. In calculating, the same factors need to be determined. The formula for calculating this is:

(Call + Dividend) + (Strike – Stock Price) / Stock Price × Time Factor = If-Called Rate of Return

Iron Condor

This type of strategy requires you to buy a call and sell a call (creating a call credit spread) and buy a put and sell a put (creating a put credit spread). Let's see how it is built-in steps. All options in this strategy have the same expiration date.

IRON CONDOR

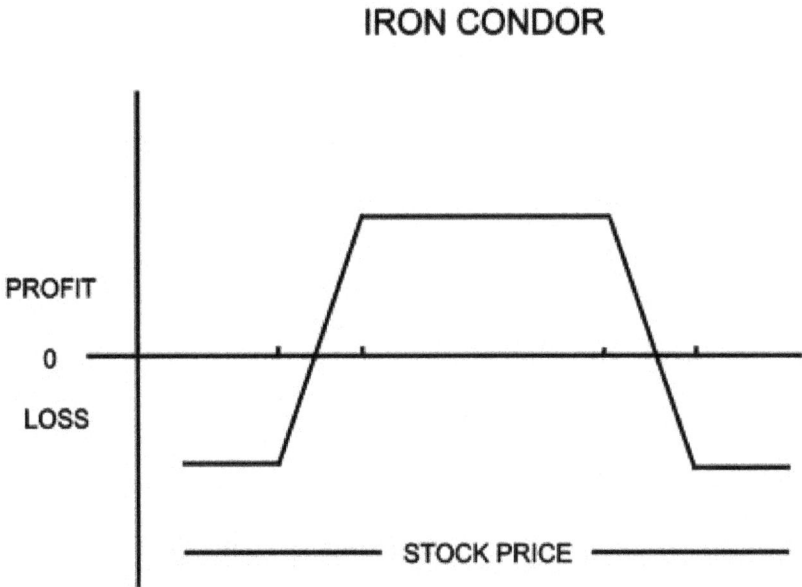

First, you pick an out of the money call price, a bit above the current share price. You sell this call. Then you buy one with a strike that is a little higher. The net difference gives you credit.

Now you pick an out of the money put option that is below the current share price. Then you sell this put option. Next, you buy an out of the money put option that has an even lower strike price. The difference here gives you another credit.

The maximum profit is the net credits. The maximum loss is given by (width of strike prices) – entry price. The broker will make you put up enough cash to cover the loss unless you have a margin account.

The narrower you make your strike prices, the lower your maximum loss, but the higher the probability that you will experience a loss. The range is set by the two options you sell, and you want the stock price to stay within those bounds.

The iron condor is a great strategy to use for monthly income. It can work exceptionally well over short time frames, like a week, since that lessens the chance of the stock going outside the range. However, many traders use a month for their iron condors.

Iron Butterfly

An iron butterfly is another strategy to use if you think the stock price will stay within a specific range. It will use four options, like the iron condor, but there will be three different strike prices.

IRON BUTTERFLY

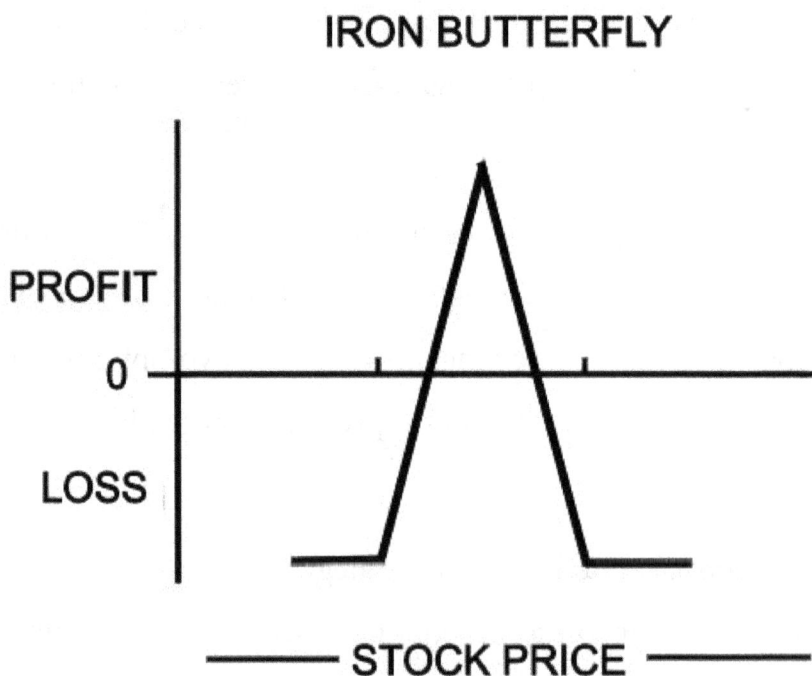

In this case, you will sell a put option and a call option with the same strike price. The strategy is to get as close to the money as possible. We will call the strike priced used the central strike. Then you set a differential price we will call x.

Like an iron condor, the profit from an iron butterfly is fixed at the net credit when you sell to open. This is given by the sum of the premiums earned from selling the at the money call and put, minus the prices paid for the out of the money options.

Long Butterfly Strategy

LONG BUTTERFLY

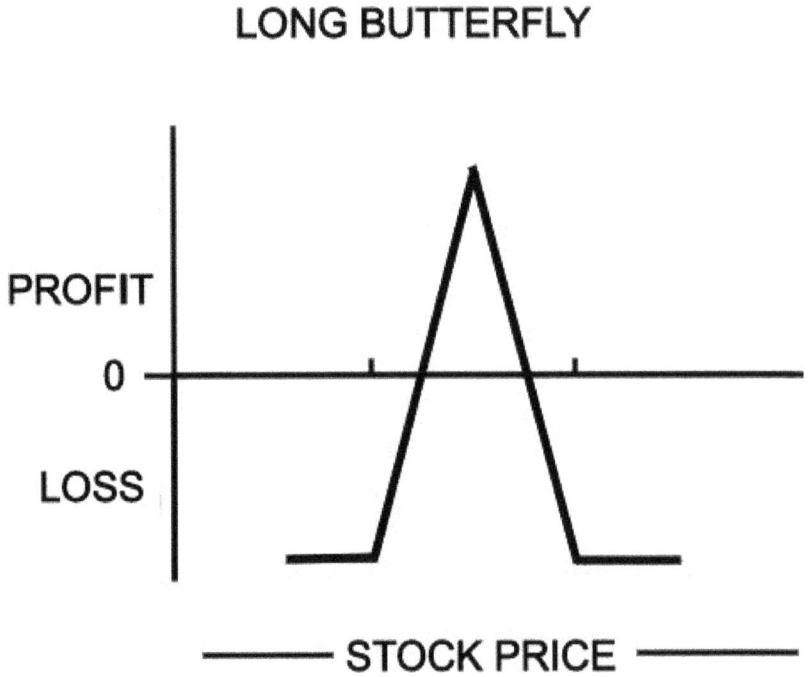

This strategy involves three parts where one put option is purchased at particular and then selling the other two options at a price lower than the buying price and purchasing one put at even lower price during a specific trading period.

Short Butterfly Strategy

SHORT BUTTERFLY

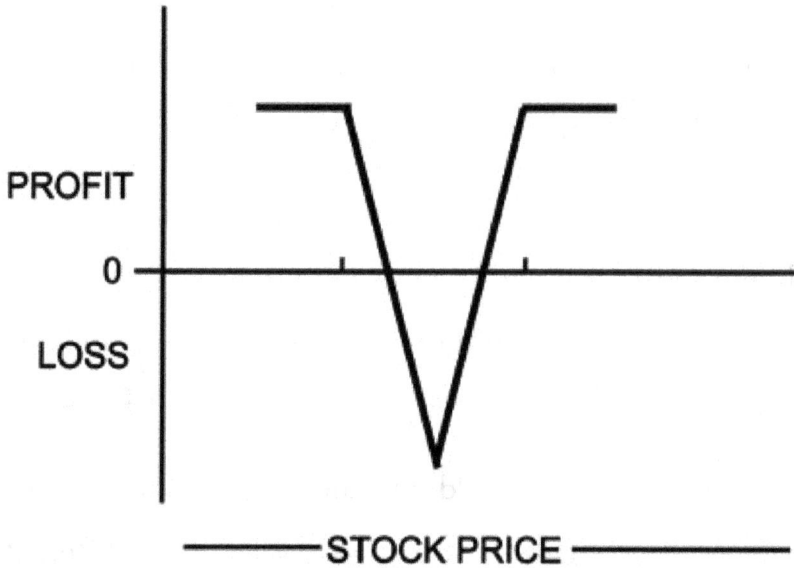

In this strategy, three parts are still involved where a put option is sold at a much higher price, and two puts are then purchased at a lower price than the purchase price, and a put option is later on sold at a much lower strike price. In both cases, all put bear the same expiration date, and the strike prices usually are equidistant, as revealed in various options trading charts. A short butterfly strategy is the opposite way of the long butterfly strategy.

CONCLUSION

All traders are very often looking for the best strategies for CFD trading on Forex, commodities, stocks, stock indices, ETFs and cryptocurrencies.

All the trading strategies we have covered in this book are only the most used and the most common ones, each of you can develop a custom one that encompasses multiple indicators together.

So a good system should include a certain degree of flexibility, which allows us to adjust it slightly in different market conditions.

Even in the case of very rigid and strict systems, or even the most complex ones, each trader should find his own way of trading and thus take advantage of it.

Finally, one should always try to develop one's own trading style, following another's rules not always just by copying and pasting, but sometimes also by trying to understand, because if there is a big chance that the copied system works, it may not always work for another trader.

The key to success is always understanding and implementing your own experience while developing the knowledge you already have.

So don't go looking for the right trading strategy, but on the contrary choose the strategy that best suits your way of trading online.

If you liked this book and want to know other aspects of online trading, the secrets or just the most important notions, we invite you to discover the other manuals in the series:

OPTIONS TRADING CRASH COURSE: FUNDAMENTALS *Everything you need to know before you start investing like a real trader*

OPTIONS TRADING CRASH COURSE: INVESTING FOR BEGINNERS *Learn how to operate in the market in the best way even if you are just a beginner*

OPTIONS TRADING CRASH COURSE: ADVANCED OPTIONS TRADING TOOLS *A simple but effective guide to operate in the market in a smart and conscious way*